AUTHOR FEARS AND HOW TO OVERCOME THEM

JOANNE MORRELL

First published in Australia 2020 with Sanguine Press

Copyright © Joanne Morrell 2020

The right of Joanne Morrell to be identified as Author of this work has been asserted by her in accordance with the Moral Right Act.

All rights reserved. No part of this book may be used or reproduced in any manner whatsoever without written permission except in the case of brief quotations embodied in critical articles and reviews.

Author Lining's books may be purchased for educational, business, or sales promotional use. For information, please email the sales team at joanne@hybridauthor.com.au

First Author Linings cover published 2020

FIRST EDITION

Cover designed by Jaz Harlow at www.dontlookdesign.com

ISBN 978-0-6485950-3-8

Also by Joanne Morrell
PRESENTED BY AUTHOR LININGS

Freelance Writing Quick Tips for Fast Success

*This book is for every author
feeling the fear
but doing what they love anyway.*

Author Fears and How to Overcome Them

This book is based on the author's personal experiences of dealing with fear as a working author and writer. Joanne Morrell is not a health professional. The contents of this book do not provide a 'cure', nor do they offer medical advice on how to eliminate unhealthy emotional behaviour.

Author Fears is full of vital information to help writers recognise and manage the common worries that arise from having a writing occupation.

In *Author Fears,* Joanne identifies doubts that hold us back from reaching our true potential. She also provides short tips on how you might overcome those doubts, without allowing fear to take over, preventing you from having the prosperous writing career you so rightfully deserve.

All definitions used throughout the book are taken from The Macquarie Dictionary unless otherwise cited.

Contents

About The Author	viii
Author Head Shot	ix
Introduction	xi
What You'll Gain by Reading This Book	xii
1. In My Experience	1
2. Confidence Fears	4
Comparisonitis	6
Exposing Yourself	8
Your Life Will Change	10
Lacking Motivation	12
Feeling Like a Fraud	14
Inadequacy	16
Being Judged by Others	18
Looking Stupid	20
You Will Never Make it as an Author	22
Self Doubt	24
People Will Laugh at Me	26
People Will Talk About Me	28
Becoming Overly Successful	30
Wasting Time in an Unknown Future	32
No One Cares About My Book	34
Who am I to Write a Book	36
3. Genre Fear Children's Fiction	38
4. Genre Fear Historical Fiction	40
5. Genre Fear Horror	42
6. Genre Fear Memoir	44
7. Genre Fears Non-Fiction	46
8. Genre Fears Romance	49
9. Craft Fears	52
Defamation	54
My Book is Too Short	56
Lack of Talent	58

Originality	60
Plagiarism	62
Being Rejected	64
Running out of Ideas	66
Self-Publishing Snobbery	69
10. Mental Health In Writers Anxiety	71
Depression	73
11. Physical Fears	75
Physical or Mental Disadvantange	77
Money	79
Unsupportive People	81
Responsibilities	84
Time	86
12. Author Lining's Traits To Succeed	88
Author Lining's Traits to Succeed	89
Freelance Writing Quick Tips for Fast Success	92
Freelance Writing Quick Tips for Fast Success	93
Acknowledgments	95

About The Author

Joanne Morrell is a writer and author based in Perth Western Australia, where she was born, but grew up in a little fishing village off the east coast of Edinburgh in Scotland.

She loves new experiences and story in all mediums: film, television and of course books. Joanne is the founder of her local book club. She is also the host and creator of The HYBRID Author Podcast which interviews industry professionals on how to forge a career independently and traditionally publishing books.
hybridauthor.com.au/podcast/

Joanne's professional writing life stems from writing children's and young adult fiction and short non fiction for authors, working as a technical scriptwriter to owning her own freelance writing business.
hybridauthor.com.au/books/

Introduction

The Macquarie Dictionary defines fear as: 'the feeling or condition of being afraid'.

Fear is seen as a bad thing. A scary thing. A thing to be anxious about. But without fear we wouldn't be able to overcome what makes us feel this way. Fear is a good thing. It keeps us alive and it makes us stronger human beings. And it's encouraging to know that you can use these fears to serve you on your writing journey.

Unavoidably, fear comes with the territory of being an author. It might be a small or large threat. However, in your author career, it is likely you will face some kind of doubt at some stage or another. As you are reading this book, I imagine you may well have experienced some sort of panic in your writing career already. I'm here to tell you it's okay. You are not alone. You can get past it.

This book is here to help.

What You'll Gain by Reading This Book

What This Book is

This book is for individuals who write, books mainly. I'm coming at it from an authorship perspective because that's the experience I have, but any writer and or creative can use my experiences to overcome any fears arising from all forms of writing.

What This Book isn't

This book is not a medical book. It does not offer medical or psychological advice. It will, however, make you realise some of what you are feeling on your writer's journey is normal, natural and a perfectly healthy part of the process all writers endure at any given stage of their writing career.

What You'll Gain by Reading This Book

An understanding that your author fears are valid. It's a comfort to know other writers feel the same way you do and are not letting fear stop them from putting themselves out there. We are all feeling the fear but doing what we love anyway.

And you can too.

It's disheartening to see so many authors develop these fears and then use them as reasons why they should not advance in their writing careers.

This book is for you.

*Of all the liars in the world,
sometimes the worst are our own fears.*
Rudyard Kipling

In My Experience

Since deciding to take my writing seriously, I have dealt with so much of what is in this book. That's why I'm writing about it. It has all come with experience at different stages of my writing career.

When I first started writing, I joined a writer's group to learn more about the art of writing. I attended workshops and events, and then I started a writing degree. In my first year of university, I independently published a children's book, middle grade. I had artwork commissioned and whilst it was a good product, I didn't have it professionally edited. When 'self-editing', I remember reading over parts of the writing that simply didn't sit right with me. Impatient to publish, I put it out there anyway, despite those initial gut feelings.

Friends and family bought my book immediately.

And I was horrified.

I remember barking at my parents because they shared an email with their friends to say I'd written a book. They were so proud of what I had achieved. But I just felt mortified.

What I was dealing with was self-doubt. I searched for answers to self-doubt and how to overcome it; I learnt a great deal about self-doubt and, as a result, *Author Fears* was 'born'!

When you've achieved something as big as having written and published a novel, telling people who are eager to know about it, "Oh, it's crap! Don't buy it!" is counter-productive. This is how I handled questions about my book: negatively. I was shy and I couldn't get behind my work because I had major self-doubt worrying about what people thought of me and my writing. It's a tough thing putting yourself out there for others to judge, and so I've included a section devoted entirely to self-doubt.

The lessons I learned from publishing that middle grade book early on were invaluable. I'm grateful I accomplished it, and even though I experienced crippling fear, I learned valuable lessons: I will always have my work professionally edited; if something doesn't sit right with my gut, I will re-write it (and re-write again) until it does; to be proud of my achievements; and not to be too hard on myself.

I've taken great care with each of my novels ever since publishing my middle grade book, so I can be confident and positive when asked about them. I do this by ensuring every element of my work is the best it can be. This all comes with experience.

I decided to write *Author Fears and How to Overcome Them* because of the many invisible and unpredictable feelings that arise in writing that novice writers generally aren't aware of until it happens to them. I wanted to write these fears and write about possible outcomes to overcome them because as your writing career progresses, different fears arise over time. This book will prepare you for the possibility of those fears invading your writing space and how to deal with them and how to tell them to bugger off.

Much of this book cross-sections into one another. I have divided them into the areas where I feel these fears dominate the most.

So let's get started.

2

Confidence Fears

AUTHOR FEAR: calling myself an author or a writer.

TITLE (definition): *a name given to someone by right of attainment.*

OVERCOME

If you are unpublished and feel uncomfortable (as I was in the beginning) to call yourself an author or a writer, you can add the adjective, 'aspiring', which gives people an understanding that you are working on being an author. You are a writer if you write for a living. You are an author if you have written a work. It doesn't matter who has seen this work or who has bought it. You wrote the words. Therefore, you are the author.

It can be challenging to accept this prestigious title. Being an author is a big deal. Writing a book is no mean feat. This fear touches on the 'imposter syndrome' section of this book. It's all linked. I've been writing for years and I still feel strange saying, *I'm a writer; I'm an author*.

Author definition: A person who writes a poem, essay or a novel.

Writer definition: A writer, journalist, or author for one's living.

REMEMBER!

If you are an author or writer, then you are these titles.

Own them.

They represent all the hard work you've put in to become what these titles represent.

Comparisonitis

AUTHOR FEAR: comparisonitis (comparing your accomplishments to others).

COMPARISON (definition): *the act of comparing.*

OVERCOME

Comparing yourself to others is something we've all done at least once in our lifetime. It's easy to look at someone and wish you looked like them or had what they have.

Comparing comes from a young age when we're taught to compare as a skill through family values, competitiveness, peer opinions, stereotypes and the media.

These feelings are generated from our own inadequacies. If we are happy with how we look, how we feel, the way we act (and generally the person we are), we could then look at others and be happy for them, admire them, learn from them and aspire to be like them, without the need to negatively compare ourselves to them.

In terms of authorship, having an author career takes time to build. Once you join the business and meet other authors, who become friends, the temptation to compare your work to the quality or success of theirs may develop. They may have already achieved what you want or become successful before you do.

If you notice you're viewing others negatively and feeling like you or your work is not as good as theirs, or you are jealous of where they are in their careers right now, write down or think about what it is they have that's making you feel this way. It could be they've published two books already and are having another one launching at the end of the month. Rather than comparing, enquire about their background.

How long have they been writing?
What does their writing routine and schedule look like?
Is there anything you can do differently to achieve the success they are experiencing?

REMEMBER!

Your life, and the amount of time, energy and effort you put into your author career, is going to differ from those around you due to varying circumstances, commitments and responsibilities.

Think of your peers as your mentors. Aspire to be like them in your own way. Find what's great and unique about you and be at peace in the world within yourself and around others, who someday may even be comparing themselves to what you have achieved, and your writing skills!

Exposing Yourself

AUTHOR FEAR: exposing yourself.

EXPOSE (definition): *to lay open.*

OVERCOME

When referring to 'exposing yourself', I'm not implying running around the streets naked, flashing people! I'm talking about what it means to expose yourself for the public, not to the public. As an aspiring author, this is not something we generally tend to think about until our book is finished. When the time comes for us to expose ourselves by publishing the work and putting it out there, is when this fear and/or feeling may generally arise.
As we get older, most of us grow.

I'm different today to when I was in my teens, to my early twenties, to the person I am now. You could say when I published my first book, it surprised some people, to the point where I even got one comment, "You've written a book? You've changed!".

Whatever you write, you are expressing your ideas, opinions, imagination and experiences in one form or another through your characters, narrative or teachings. On some level, whether you mean to or not, you are exposing a part of you that others might never have seen before. This can be both scary and wonderful at the same time.

The best way to get a handle on exposing yourself is to identify with the main themes of your work and your reasons for what you are writing. Understanding your work's purpose is all you need in response to introducing depths of yourself to others. By doing so, you will connect with like-minded people on a new level, regardless of whether they are not the same people you associated with before. These are the people for you *now*.

REMEMBER!

Your book is not for everyone and you don't need to justify your work to anyone.

Overcome exposing yourself.

Be true to the *you* of *now*.

Your Life Will Change

AUTHOR FEAR: your life will change.

CHANGE (definition): *to make or become different.*

OVERCOME

When writing a book, people believe (or hope) their life will change. And generally, it will. Maybe not financially or recognitionally. But because of the fact you've written a book, that's what's changed. It's a massive achievement! And you should be proud, no matter the outcome.

I feel I have changed after each book I've written. I've gained more understanding on a subject or learned something new about myself. How much your life will change depends on what you do with your book, by the way of publishing it, marketing it and getting on with the next one. You might discover writing perhaps isn't for you.

Whatever you decide is okay.

After you write a book, change in some form is something you will face as an author.

Some people view change negatively. It's easy to get comfortable in yourself and your daily routines. Change catapults uncertainty. It's scary because we don't know if it's going to be good or bad. Sometimes change is forced upon us and even though it appears negative, there are always reasons behind change. If a person has a heart attack, they must change to live a healthier life if they want to reduce the risk of having another one; or if a person wants to earn more money, they may change careers. As we take on responsibilities, we must change our behaviour to match what is required of us, or else we will become stagnant.

- What are some of the changes you foresee with your publishing plan?
- How will you prepare yourself for these changes?

REMEMBER!

Regard change as a good thing. It can be scary, but don't let it stop you.

Do it anyway and find out for yourself.

Lacking Motivation

AUTHOR FEAR: lacking motivation.

MOTIVATION (definition): *ambitious, determined, energetic.*

OVERCOME

Your idea is amazing and you're pumped! The pages are filling up fast. However, at some point many writers hit a wall and run out of steam. There are many reasons why a writer stops writing. It can be due to researching further, working through plot holes, character dilemmas or simply real life getting in the way of your time to write.

Writing is work. That, in itself, can cause individuals to avoid putting in the hours. Most writers know all about procrastination and will find anything else to do, but write. It can be fun, thinking, creating and constructing, but it is your butt in front of the computer, writing pad (or however you get your words down) that matters the most. Sometimes getting to that space can be the biggest challenge of all.

I struggled for years to write regularly. It wasn't that I didn't want to, but sometimes it's hard to motivate yourself to do things, especially if you have a family, busy life and other commitments taking up your energy and time; writing has to work somewhere in amongst these obligations. And it can be hard to keep up the momentum.

Find what motivates you to write. For me, it was when another year ticked by and I was no further forward with my manuscript. I said to myself, "Jo, if you ever want to have a career as an author, you need to get yourself together and focus. Get the writing done!" What's more important? So, I made writing a priority. I focused on getting my book finished. Every struggle and every push to do my writing has resulted in me getting further, writing more, becoming motivated to the point now where I just do it.

REMEMBER!

Find what motivates you and use it to get the work done.

Feeling Like a Fraud

AUTHOR FEAR: feeling like a fraud.

IMPOSTER SYNDROME:
en.wikipedia.org/wiki/Impostor_syndrome

Impostor syndrome (also known as impostor phenomenon, impostorism, fraud syndrome or the impostor experience) is a psychological pattern in which an individual doubts their accomplishments and has a persistent internalized fear of being exposed as a "fraud".[1] Despite external evidence of their competence, those experiencing this phenomenon remain convinced that they are frauds, and do not deserve all they have achieved.

OVERCOME

In *Freelance Writing Quick Tips for Fast Success,* I touch on a time when I dealt with Imposter Syndrome:

'After I graduated, I began applying for the kind of jobs from which

I used to make a living; office work, retail, even hospitality. It was what I knew. Universities don't necessarily teach you how to shift your mindset to a self-starter one. I didn't feel qualified to apply for jobs that might use the knowledge I'd just obtained in my writing degree. I worried I might look like a fool, or worse, do a poor job. I had imposter syndrome and felt like a fraud for a few years.

And it held me back!'

REMEMBER!

Eventually, as I gained experience in my field and started earning a living from my writing, the imposter syndrome slowly started to fade away. My confidence in myself and my abilities as a writer arrived. I would never look back at my past professions as a 'go to' to earn money (as I had done when I graduated). I always look at writing opportunities or how I can earn a living around my writing.

Inadequacy

AUTHOR FEAR: inadequacy.

INADEQUACY (definition): not good enough.https://dictionary.cambridge.org/dictionary/english/inadequate

OVERCOME

If you believe you are not good enough, I encourage you to determine what it is about you or your writing that you deem 'not good enough'.

I'm very much a feelings person. I'm what I call a gut writer. I write with my gut ever since publishing my first novel. Inadequacy took a hold of me when publishing this first novel.

I should have engaged the services of a professional editor to help me smooth out those couple of paragraphs that didn't feel right, but I skipped over them. Now, when I'm writing and I feel something isn't right, I work on it until I feel it is right. And I will always have my work edited by a professional!

Write down what it is that makes you think you are not good enough. If it's your writing skills, that's easily fixed; attend a workshop or take a course. Whatever it is you require to feel adequate, embrace it. Start believing you and your writing are enough!

My way of thinking is, "Why not me?"

REMEMBER!

It can be you. You are enough. And you can be good enough if you practise, apply and be patient.

Being Judged by Others

AUTHOR FEAR: being judged by others.

JUDGED (definition): to form a judgement or opinion.

OVERCOME

This fear has been briefly touched upon in the 'people will laugh at me' and 'looking stupid' sections. Unfortunately, this fear is unavoidable in this business and in any creative outlet, for that matter. Your work is created and perceived by the public. People who engage with it will form an opinion. These judgements can be good or bad or both.

And you need to be fine with that.

There was a conversation thread on Twitter I was following recently with a rather well-known, young adult author. They received a review of their novel from an adult who dubbed the book 'too juvenile'. This annoyed the author as the book is for a young audience. Their concern was this review might deter younger readers from wanting to read the book as an adult had deemed it 'juvenile'.

REMEMBER!

Sometimes you will be judged unfairly and not necessarily by your target audience. Expect to be judged; embrace the judgements. Work through them. And move on. Write some more.

Everyone has their own opinion. Everyone has different tastes.

And always keep writing!

Looking Stupid

AUTHOR FEAR: looking stupid.

FOOLISH (definition): silly or stupid.

OVERCOME

I often become anxious around thinking I'm going to make a fool of myself in front of people. I'm less concerned these days, as I'm quite confident if I did make myself look silly, I'd just laugh it off, or make a joke about it. I always remind myself when I do workshops or speak, I trust the attendees are intelligent and non-judgemental people who understand how difficult it is to stand up in front of a bunch of people and talk, let alone teach. I think about how I feel watching someone present. If I spot they are nervous, I feel compassion towards them. Most importantly, I don't judge them for it. People are understanding. I know my enthusiasm for what I'm speaking about or teaching outweighs any worries of looking stupid.

To overcome feeling this way, be prepared. If you are organised with the session you are going to conduct and have practised your run through, you will feel confident about how the workshop will progress. Being prepared for mishaps, such as technology faults, will also help with extinguishing feelings like you are going to 'look stupid'.

What the hell is 'looking stupid' anyway? Is it mumbling? Or is it forgetting what you are going to say? Have items in place like prompt cards. It's okay to use aids when you are first starting out. In fact, I'd even encourage you to use cards. It's going to make you a better and more confident presenter or writer.

REMEMBER!

Do what you've got to do to quiet your mind and build confidence in the beginning. The better you become, the fewer aids you will need.

You Will Never Make it as an Author

AUTHOR FEAR: you will never make it as an author.

FAILURE (definition): something or someone who does not succeed.

OVERCOME

Define what 'making it as an author' means to you; everyone's idea of 'making it' will differ from one another:

Is it to have a career as an author?
Earn money from being an author?
Support yourself or your family as an author?
Or is making it as an author about writing books and having people read them?
Or all the above?

As the definition of career states, having an author career is a general progress of a person's lifework throughout their entire existence. It's not: *write one book and get rich; never write again.* It's about creating and building a body of work over a lifetime. Income can be involved in this process, so in order to accomplish your goals, you may well need to earn from your writing.

If money is how you dub success, how much will you need to be successful?
Personally, I don't believe in failure. I could look at the first book I ever published and say that was a failure. But it wasn't. I learned many lessons which have helped me greatly in my career. And so, the way I see it, I have succeeded in a different way than I originally envisioned. Sometimes what we want doesn't work but we gain something else we never knew we needed in its place.

REMEMBER!

What matters to you might not matter to most. Start by defining this fear to meet your own aspirations and goals.

And go kick its scrawny little ass!

Self Doubt

AUTHOR FEAR: Self doubt

SELF-DOUBT (definition): A lack of faith in oneself.

OVERCOME

Self-doubt. My old frenemy. It's probably the biggest fear most writers face at all stages of their career. Self-doubt visits often and unlike in the beginning of my writing life, I now welcome self-doubt.

I believe self-doubt is like a rite of passage. You are not an author until you've dealt with a little side of self-doubt. If there's no self-doubt, there's no doing it right.
At least once in our lifetime, I'm sure every one of us has dealt with self-doubt.

- Embrace it
- Write it down

- Acknowledge the feelings
- Then get over them and release

We all often have days where we think our writing shines, then the next, it's utter garbage. The voice of self-doubt creeps in.

You can't do this
Your writing sucks
You're wasting your time

Quieten this voice down by believing in yourself and your abilities as a writer. Just write. Your editor will help make your writing better. Time and writing more will also help. Learning your craft will help improve your writing.

REMEMBER!

Instead of choosing to believe your writing is rubbish, choose to believe it's great.

And it will be.

People Will Laugh at Me

AUTHOR FEAR: People will laugh at me

MOCK (definition): To attack with ridicule.

OVERCOME

As an author, sometimes you might find you are invited to present.

During my studies at university as part of a presentations unit I was undertaking about speaking publicly, I had to stand up and talk about an idea. I spoke about the book I'd published in my first year of study. I was nervous. I was worried what people would think of me and the self-published book I held in my hands. But, I did it anyway. I respectfully remember the response and hold in my mind to revisit any time this fear rears its ugly head. People were genuinely interested and a few students even made a point of coming up to me afterwards, telling me they were writers too, which was amazing.

Not only did people *not* laugh at me; they *connected* with me. You have to put yourself out there to face your fear and make the realisation, fear is nothing more than *false evidence appearing real*. It's in your head.

Make a list of the kinds of things you think people might laugh at you about, then write what you can do to limit your worries.

Example: What I'm wearing, how I look. Be yourself, wear what feels comfortable. This is your style, so own it.

REMEMBER!

Whatever the event you are conducting, the audience will be people who are interested in what you have to say. They've not come to judge and ridicule you. They've come to learn from you and support you.

People Will Talk About Me

AUTHOR FEAR: People will talk about me

GOSSIP (definition): Idle talk, especially about the affairs of others.

OVERCOME

Whether you are a writer or not, people will always talk about people behind their back. It's a given. Whether it comes from a place of love or a place of hostility, all you need to do is focus on your next book. Your writing. You can only get better. Don't pay attention to what's negatively being said about you, your work, in person or in the media. It's entirely up to you how much of it you want to take in. You never know, some of it might even be constructive!

Keep in mind, not everyone is going to love your work. Just like your work is not meant for everyone. The sooner you realise this and make peace with it, the calmer your writing life will become.

I didn't receive any feedback from my first book. And to me, the silence said it all. But what I now realise about that book is it was bought by my friends and family, not my target audience (children of middle grade, ages 8-12) or lovers of the genre.

REMEMBER!

Reviews of our work are important to gain awareness and start a conversation. We're all entitled to an opinion whether it's negative or positive. You're in charge of what you do with these opinions.

Becoming Overly Successful

AUTHOR FEAR: Becoming overly successful

SUCCESS (definition): The gaining of wealth, position or the like.

OVERCOME

Whilst it seems success is what most authors are chasing, it can be viewed as a negative. With extreme success, comes money and power. Some people can change when this comes into play, and not necessarily for the better. We never know how successful our work will become until we put it out there. Instantly thrown into the spotlight, we humble authors who write at home may struggle with attention, should we hit 'the big time'.

Luckily for us, we are authors, not actors.

Authors are encouraged to socialise and network with other industry professionals and individuals who share the same passions as you, as well as meeting readers and fans of your work (which can be a major boost to self-confidence hearing all the nice comments people have to say about your work).

If you become famous and find yourself thrust into the limelight, help is available: coaches, managers and agents. These professionals work in the business and can advise you on public appearances. So, don't stress too much on this one; instead, define what success means to you:

- Is it to have a fan base of readers who love your book no matter how big or small?
- Is it to see your book in a book shop?
- Is it simply to hold your book in your hands or to earn a living from it?
- Is it to have a long career as an author and support your entire family?

REMEMBER!

Whatever success means to you, work it out, understand it, stick to it and align all your authorship business endeavours against it.

Wasting Time in an Unknown Future

AUTHOR FEAR: Wasting time in an unknown future

UNCERTAIN (definition): not clearly or precisely determined; indefinite; unknown.
www.dictionary.com

OVERCOME

Writing a book takes time. It takes effort, dedication and hard work. Depending on what outcome you are hoping to achieve, let's take a look at this from a professional avenue: it's your time in exchange for an uncertain future as an author. I guess you should be asking yourself if it is worth your time and effort? Many authors mention the financial gains are not worth the return on investment (ROI) for the amount of work they put in. The difference being, they love the work. It outweighs the financial rewards, so they do it anyway.

I want to write my books and I want to make money. I consider authorship as a career. I love it, but I'm not solely doing it because I love it. It's hard work and more than just a hobby. It's what I want to do with my time 24/7, and to do that I have to earn a living from it. So, it may be 10-20 books down the track before I start earning the type of income I require to financially support my family. But I'm in this for as long as it takes.

REMEMBER!

It may be an uncertain future in the beginning, but it won't be forever, if you stick with it and keep writing.

There are many individuals earning a fabulous living from their writing and you can be one of them!

No One Cares About My Book

AUTHOR FEAR: No one cares about my book.

UNCONCERNED (definition): To be concerned.

OVERCOME

This statement is simply not true. *You* care about your book. And so, it's your job to work out how to get others to care about your book too.

Regardless of whether you are independently published or traditionally published, I believe it is your responsibility to get others to care about your book.

So, who are these 'others', the people who care about your book? Well, it's the people you write the book for: your target audience. You can work with your publisher or if you are the publisher, you can implement a marketing plan to ensure you reach people. In doing so, always remember people have different tastes and your book is not for everyone. Pinpoint the themes in the book and target the individuals who would care about them.

Example: My middle grade novel, *Popcorn Girl*, contains heavy themes of popcorn. I'm thinking cinemas where great stories are told visually. I'm thinking of the setting (which is Iowa) and the places that sell popcorn in restaurants, as a way of thinking outside of the box.

My non-fiction books are about the physical and emotional aspects of authorship. At festivals, writing groups, libraries, and the like, I'll find people who share my interest in writing and meet aspiring writers who might benefit from my experience.

REMEMBER!

Your work is important. If you care enough about it, you'll find the 'others' who care about it too.

Who am I to Write a Book

AUTHOR FEAR: who am *I* to write a book?

STATUS (definition): condition, position, or standing socially, professionally, or otherwise.

OVERCOME

Who is **anybody** to write a book?

A person with an idea, an experience or an expert on a certain subject, that's who. I'm a firm believer we can do just about anything our hearts desire. It may take some longer than others, but if you are willing to put the time, effort and work into making what you want to happen, then there's every reason everything you want can be yours.

I believe the notion of books being linked to intelligence is where this fear grows. I didn't finish high school, so I can relate to this stigma. But since studying for many years earning diplomas, certificates and a Bachelors in Writing, this fear has cut all ties with me.

You don't need to have these qualifications to write a book. I certainly didn't when I first started out. That's why I went on to study the subject of writing in the first place. It was a desire. An interest. And only through following this hobby did I decide to take it seriously and make the realisation writing has always been a factor in my life, from a very young age.

A basic understanding of the English language, a brief set of editing skills and an understanding of a story arc are all that's required to get you started in novel writing.

REMEMBER!

You have a brain. You have a story to tell. You have an imagination. You have an idea. *That's who you are to write a book.* Intelligence comes into it, but you don't need a PhD to write. You simply have to get started. As the old saying goes, 'everyone has a book in them.' We all have a story to tell. Your entire existence is one, big, long story.

It's up to you, the writer, to make it interesting.

3

Genre Fear Children's Fiction

AUTHOR FEAR: Not writing for the appropriate age group

AGE (definition): The length of time of someone's existence

OVERCOME

When writing for children you need to consider what themes and use of language are appropriate for the intended age of your young audience. For instance, content of a sexual nature wouldn't appear in a young reader's book; nor would lengthy, unpronounceable words above the reader's level of comprehension. Swear words in a picture book for instance (unless written for adults) would not go down well.
In the past, I've often felt like the writing in my children's fiction is too advanced for the intended target age group. Don't dwell on this too much (as I did). It's a waste of your precious writing time!

Instead, write the story you want to write.

REMEMBER!

Leave it up to your publisher and or editor as to how the language should be suited to your determined audience.

- If I've learned anything, it's that every publishing house is different. They will market your story to suit their style. So, leave these details up to them.

If you are the publisher, then it is up to you to do your research. Once you have written your story, think about the content and discover where it would best fit in the market. Tweak appropriately for your book's maximum performance.

4

Genre Fear Historical Fiction

AUTHOR FEAR: Providing incorrect historical information

ALLEDGED (definition): To assert without proof

OVERCOME

A writer friend of mine who writes historical fiction in their novels mentioned that when researching, they often come across conflicting information with the histories they are investigating. The way to overcome this is by making sure you're acquiring information from a reliable and valued source, such as a scholarly review, rather than a hobby website.
Depending on the time period, facts can be wrong – there's no doubt about that. Writing as closely as possible to the truth with what you've learned is the only way to overcome this worry. You can also make a note in the front of your book matter, stating: *These facts are to the best of my knowledge researched from* . . . This should protect you if any issues arise with incorrect facts and data, going forward.

REMEMBER!

If you are going down the traditionally published route, then it is the publishing editor's job to check all your facts before publication. If you are self-publishing, it is your responsibility. Although you may hire the services of a freelance editor, be prepared to pay quite a bit extra to have your facts checked on your behalf, as this is a timely process depending on the type of work.

5

Genre Fear Horror

AUTHOR FEAR: people thinking you are dark and weird.

WEIRD (definition): odd or queer.

HORROR (definition): great fear.

OVERCOME

Writing horror is writing what others fear. That's the point. To scare people. To take the ordinary and turn it into a nightmare. You might be worried how people will perceive you if you write truly awful or dark stuff. All you need say is that it's a part of the genre for whom you write. You write to market, which is horror. They wouldn't expect you to write a fluffy romance if you were writing horror. This is what you enjoy. These are your stories and characters (but they are not you).
Wherever your inspiration lies (either through research or from your own distresses), you don't need to justify your story to those few people who hold this view. They are not your fan base. They

obviously don't appreciate the genre for what it is. Therefore, I wouldn't hold their opinion in high regard. You want to find the masses who love what you do and appreciate your art for what it is.

Think of horror as catharsis. Release your worst nightmares upon the world and provide people with the hope to survive through them.

(Horror can have a happy ending too.)

REMEMBER!

They say **everyone** has a dark side.

Find your people.

Own your ideas.

6

Genre Fear Memoir

AUTHOR FEAR: writing about people you know.

ACQUAINTANCE (definition): person(s) known to one, but not intimately.

OVERCOME

It would be difficult not to include one of these people above when writing memoir. To write about people you know can be challenging and worrying. What might they think of the way you portray certain events or the way you describe them?

As a first step, I believe you need to map out how you are going to depict someone or something. Gaining permission from the person you are writing about is imperative, if you don't want to attract a bunch of lawsuits down the track. Because the way you remember things from the past will always be different from the way someone else who witnessed the same thing remembers. The way you will tell a story or a turn of events is always going to vary from how others might relay the same happenings.

REMEMBER!

Make sure you are well-versed in all aspects of writing memoir – how to go about it and what legal advice you need to be aware of. Seek help from your local Copyright Council or Arts Community Law Practice or Society of Authors, if applicable.

7

Genre Fears Non-Fiction

AUTHOR FEAR: scared to voice your opinion.

QUIET (definition): restrained in speech or manner.

OVERCOME

Writing non-fiction is, in some way, giving your advice, telling a story or sharing your opinion on a matter. The way you might deal with this is by lightly taking on a tone which implies a certain notion, rather than jamming the information down people's throats assertively, as if it was the only option and no other exists.

It can be challenging to speak your mind. There might be backlash. People might not agree with your thoughts; you might be on your own in your views.

Make peace with the notion: *people will either agree with what you've got to say or they won't*. Focus on the message you want to deliver and the way you want to drive it without causing negative impact.

Being open to the consideration of others' experiences and opinions facilitates a receiving of minds and vice versa.

REMEMBER!

Make your opinions valid, interesting and non-aggressive. But make them! Because how you feel about something matters. Your voice matters, even if it's different from everyone else. That's what writing's all about, isn't it? You have a distinctive voice, so let it shine through your writing.

AUTHOR FEAR: Scared of not knowing enough about a topic.

UNINFORMED (definition): Not having or showing awareness or understanding of the facts.
(Dictionary.com)

OVERCOME

If you feel you don't know enough about a subject to write about it or talk about it, this can be easily fixed. Research, research, research! You can find out as much (or as little) as you like about almost anything at your local library or online. Then you can put your own spin on it; just make sure what you are researching is from a reputable source.

If you are concerned people will give you backlash about your topic, practise your responses to questions you feel uncertain about or simply state up front in your book or talk:

"I'm not an expert on this subject, but I have written about my experiences ... which I would like to share with others."

Add a disclosure statement at the beginning of your book. For example, *I am not a medical practitioner. This is not a book where you will seek medical advice for having unhelpful thoughts. I can only answer from my heart.*

REMEMBER!

Be wary you're not hiding in research. This fear can often stall you from moving on from the knowledge part of the process to the most important step: getting on with the writing.

8

Genre Fears Romance

AUTHOR FEAR: your story is clichéd.

CLICHÉ (definition): a trite, stereotyped expression, idea or practice.

OVERCOME

We all know one scenario in a romance: someone is going to fall in love. Readers of this genre expect that. That's why they read these books; romance is what they want. If you feel your story is too similar to what's been done before, then think about what you could do differently from your average love triangle; perfect characters, bad boy goes for good girl scenario. Even if you have included one of these, the way you tell a story is going to be different from the way someone else tells it.

It's okay to write romance the way it has been 'tried and tested', as long as your readers are left with a warm, fuzzy feeling at the end, or balling their eyes out from an everlasting dying romance. However, if you can do it differently, do it.

Think about your own loves in life, if any, or the people around you.

- How did they meet?
- How do they behave?
- What is their story?

REMEMBER!

Even if you believe readers want a fairy tale, you can still create one based upon real life.

Clichés in romance are:

- Love at first sight
- Childhood best friends fall in love
- High school sweethearts reunite
- Love triangles
- Woman scorned
- Artificial low substance characters
- The love story is the only thing happening

AUTHOR FEAR: Writing Cheesy Romance

CHEESY (definition): Something that is overly cute, sweet, sentimental. In a positive way, yet over the top or trying too hard.

urbandictionary.com/define.php?term=Cheesy

OVERCOME

Consider your love life. The people around you. How many couples do you know who gush over each other or constantly talk about one another or think about each other all day long or call each other a million times because they missed one another? Hey, there might be a few. But is it real or is it fake? And by 'fake' I mean putting on a show for the benefit of others, where as behind closed doors, their lives are less than perfect.

You can still write a romance touching on these gestures and certainly it might be why people read romance in the first place. Edging the fine line of 'less is more' might be a way to avoid the 'ick' factor.

The way to keep track of whether your romance is borderline or full-blown stinky blue cheese is by counting: how many interactions your characters have and what they do in these moments. Do they touch or stare longingly into each other's eyes?

REMEMBER!

Make sure you don't have your protagonist thinking only about their love interest. What else is going on in the story that showcases this love to be 'awe' – not 'ick'?

9

Craft Fears

AUTHOR FEAR: criticism.

CRITICISE (definition): to make judgements as to merits and faults; to find faults.

OVERCOME

As writers, we will all have our writing critiqued at one point or another, whether that be by a friend, a group or a professional. In the beginning, we want to know what works and what doesn't with our words so we can make it the best it can be, before publication. What's hard to take is hearing criticism after your work is finished and put out into the world. But it falls to you for how you take the good with the bad. It's about accepting not everyone will love your work. And being okay with that.

If you want to be a writer, expect to be criticised. It comes with the territory. You can choose how you use critiques. You can take them to heart; let them destroy you. Or you can use them to improve.

Accept everyone is entitled to their own opinions. You're a writer – you can take it!

REMEMBER!

Some people offer constructive criticism, whilst others only provide unhelpful feedback. So, don't get hung up on the criticisms of others because everyone sees things differently.

Defamation

AUTHOR FEAR: defamation.

DEFAME (definition): to attack the good name or reputation of, as by uttering or publishing maliciously anything injurious, slander.

OVERCOME

We all filter information differently. The way I perceive something is different from the way you would understand something because we are two different people. However, the way you write about another person could come across negatively.

If you feel you are in breach of writing harmful content about an individual, it may serve you to have your work checked by a professional to make sure what you are writing is not defaming the person you are writing about.

Seek advice from a lawyer if you believe you are in breach of defamation. Your local Arts Law Community Centre (if you have one) is an even better place to start. These lawyers are trained to look after the arts community in such matters as defamation.

If you are traditionally published, your publishing house and their editorial team should be able to determine whether your work is defaming another or not. If you are independently publishing, it falls upon you.

REMEMBER!

Be cautious whenever you are writing about living people and have your work checked if you have the slightest doubt you may be defaming someone.

My Book is Too Short

AUTHOR FEAR: my book is too short.

LESS (definition): smaller in size amount or extent.

OVERCOME

You know the sayings: *less is more* and *good things come in small packages?* Both are true. Worrying whether your book is too short is wasteful energy. There is a market for short books: novellas, short stories and flash fiction.

The benefits of writing a short work are plentiful and suit the needs of today's busy readers. They want to consume information fast; they hold short attention spans. There has never been a better time for short, snappy content. This doesn't mean you know less about a subject. It just means you don't waffle. I have often chosen the thin spine of a topic over a thick spine because I want to learn quickly.

When I write, I always have less material than more. I generally have to go back and flesh out my words. I'd never 'stuff a book' to a reach word count. I generally have an approximate number of words I believe the book will comprise, and it generally falls short (no pun intended).

REMEMBER!

Everyone has a preference; short is a preference too.

Lack of Talent

AUTHOR FEAR: lack of Talent.

TALENT (definition): special natural ability.

OVERCOME

How do you become good at something? You practise, that's how. You keep doing it until you get better and better and better at it. Some people might be born with the natural ability to entertain, tell a story or write, while others have to work harder at it to realise their true potential and reach their goals.

And just because you might have to work harder at learning to write because it doesn't come easily to you, doesn't mean you aren't a writer and doesn't mean you shouldn't be chasing this dream. It will mean so much more to you when all your hard work pays off. Because you earned it.

REMEMBER!

Like any job or career, no one starts outstanding. Everyone is a learner in the beginning. Expect to grow and keep at it. Talent will come the more you write; the more you learn; the more you understand and develop your voice and what it is you are trying to say.

I've heard many debates over talent and whether or not it's real. What I do know is writing is a skill and not just an act. Determination, dedication and motivation are all part of that skill. Talent will only take you so far.

Originality

AUTHOR FEAR: originality.

ORIGINAL (definition): fresh, novel.

OVERCOME

Ideas for stories may have been 'done to death'. But know this: *no one person is ever going to write the same or tell the same story in the way that you do, because you are you.*

If you gave a classroom full of people the idea of a story – let's say 'a magic wizard goes to school', that classroom will have the same concept to work with, but no one person in that class will produce the same story told in the same manner. There might be the same concepts but they won't be the same story. So, don't stress too much about being original. You already are!

You can push yourself to 'think outside the box' and how you could do things differently. But don't let this be a big issue holding you back from writing. Write, and the ideas will come. Your experiences and take on things are different from everyone else.

REMEMBER!

What makes you original and unique from others is *you*.

Write what you want to write, free of any doubts. Let the words speak for themselves; see what evolves on the page. Once the work is complete, you can assess your work and write down the aspects you believe make your work unoriginal: stereotypical characters and settings, or stories that are similar to others you've heard. Think of how you can make it original after you've written what needs to be said first.

Don't get bogged down with these details. Always write first and then think later.

Plagiarism

AUTHOR FEAR: my work being stolen.

PLAGARISM (definition): a piece of writing, music or art appropriated or commissioned from another and passed off as one's own.

OVERCOME

You spend a long time perfecting your words. It can be daunting when the time comes to start sending your work out. How would you ever know if someone stole something of yours unless it hit the big time? How would you be able to prove it?

Think of the outfit you are sending your work to. Do your research: Are they a reputable company or publisher? If they are, it's unlikely these are the types of people who would want to steal your work.

The ways to prove your manuscript or words are yours are by:

- Email your documents to yourself, as proof.
- Use Software, like *Scrivener*, which shows the date and time a work is modified and which can serve as a record.
- Keep **all** your drafts (every single one of them!).

REMEMBER!

Ideas are not copyrighted. Works are. In Australia, we are lucky to have The Copyright Council of Australia to help with all our copyright queries. Check what organisations you have in place for your rights in your country.

If you don't want to have your ideas stolen, keep them to yourself until you have a finished work. However, as touched upon in the 'originality' section, no one person will write the same idea, word for word; we are all different.

In some countries, you have to register your copyright. Check to make sure what you need to do to protect your work before you either show or send it to anyone! If someone steals your actual writing, this is called plagiarism. And it's illegal, so report it.

Being Rejected

AUTHOR FEAR: being rejected.

REJECT (definition): to refuse to have, take or recognise.

OVERCOME

Unlike most of the fears in this book, rejection is a fear you can almost guarantee you will be up against if you want to have a career as a writer. Nobody wants to be rejected. And maybe you might not. If you 'independently publish', you don't have to be rejected time and time again; you have the option to take your publishing efforts into your control.

But if you are choosing the traditional path (where rejection is almost a given), change the word 'rejection'. Instead, refer to it as: 'not at this time'.

It's easy for us to take rejection to heart, thinking our work is rubbish or we're not good enough. In reality, publishers receive a massive number of manuscripts each week.

This industry is fierce and competitive which shouldn't deter you, but fuel you to go after what you want harder and faster than ever before. Publishers only have a certain number of books they can accept in a particular genre. They also have to look after the author list they have already established.

A rejection from a publisher could be because your story is too similar to something they've just produced and isn't ready for them quite yet. They also have to look at your manuscript as a whole and consider how much work your book needs, editing wise, and whether they have enough time in their schedule to produce it.

REMEMBER!

When you receive a rejection, realise many factors come into play. It's not always about the work not being good enough. It's many more things. And remember, with each 'no', you are one step closer to a 'yes'.

Don't take it too personally. Just because it's a 'NOT right now', doesn't mean it's a 'NEVER'.

Running out of Ideas

AUTHOR FEAR: running out of ideas.

IDEA (definition): any conception or new thought resulting from mental understanding or activity.

OVERCOME

I'm fortunate enough to have ideas, often. I have a list of them I need to write in order as they materialise to me. For some, ideas don't come so easy. What I have found is ideas emerge from having my own experiences. I've never actually sat down and tried to come up with an idea to write a book. All my books have an element in them I can relate to, whether it be where they are set, a certain character or scenario.

The common worries behind ideas are:

- not having enough ideas;

- not writing the right idea;
- ideas not being good enough; and
- having ideas similar to everyone else.

If you are a 'pantser' (someone who writes 'by the seat of their pants') like me, often the ideas we start a book with can turn into something else as we go along.

If you truly can't come up with an idea from anything you've ever experienced or want to write about, try playing around with some fun games that will generate an idea for you. Get five sheets of paper, write headings on them: characters, themes, settings, emotions and backstory. Write 20 choices on paper for each one. If you are stuck, consider the genre you want to write in and apply options in relation to that genre.

For example:

- *Fantasy*
- *Character*: a warlock.
- *Themes*: sexual harassment.
- *Setting*: a dragon's layer.
- *Emotions*: excitement.
- *Backstory*: dismissed from the warlock navy and is a secret cross-dresser.

And, just start writing. An idea should come from these elements. Do it just for fun and see what happens. You'll be surprised.

REMEMBER!

Ideas come from all around us:

- what people say;
- how people behave; and
- answers to problems or questions we might have on a certain subject.

Fine tune your observation skills and you'll be inundated with ideas.

Self-Publishing Snobbery

AUTHOR FEAR: self-publishing snobbery.

SNOB (definition): someone who affects social importance and exclusiveness.

OVERCOME

Self-publishing attracted a great deal of stigma in the past. Once upon a time, it was regarded as not being good enough to secure a traditional deal; the easy option. But the writers who are business-minded recognise the model for what it is: a way to gain full control over your work and reap the benefits in the process.

Sure, these independent publishing platforms allow anybody to publish their work, which means there is no filter and there are some inferior books floating around out there. I can argue there are also some crappy traditionally published works out there too. Have you ever read a book and thought, "Jeez! How did *that* get published?"

Of course, there are 'chancers' who try to make a buck from a bad product. But as the industry changes so fast, these blaggers disappear over time. The true professionals stand their ground, adapt and move forward. Their work sells through word of mouth and good marketing practice and because their work is good.

Readers and non-writer people who buy books don't generally care where or who a book is published by as long as it's meeting a need, doing its job properly by fulfilling its purpose, such as:

- **Fiction**: the reader escaped or was entertained.
- **Non-fiction**: provided useful self-help advice or information on a subject matter.

REMEMBER!

As long as you are investing in making a product as good as it can be by having your work professionally edited, getting a professional cover design and being professional about publishing as a business, you can ignore any self-publishing snobbery you may come up against. Instead, be proud of your self-publishing efforts and think of your reasons for wanting to self-publish in the first place.

Are you meeting your needs by publishing this way?

For me, I wanted to put out my own non-fiction as I wanted to have full control over it. On the other hand, with my children's fiction, I was more inclined to source a traditional publisher, as I wanted that experience as well as that credibility under my belt.

10

Mental Health In Writers
Anxiety

As someone who has experienced both anxiety and depression through various stages of my life, I'm making mention of it here because I think it's important. As writers, we live inside our heads most of the time, and it can be very hard to deal with these fears and or negative thoughts which summon negative symptoms that can evolve from being a writer working in isolation.

There are also many more positive aspects about this industry that I choose to focus on instead. That's why I've written this book, to remind myself that I have felt these things and will inevitably feel them again. I've faced them and kept going. I'm so glad I did and I hope others will too.

Anxiety is a mental illness and one I struggled with the most. There are different types. Once I realised what it was I was experiencing (which, according to my therapist at the time, was social and generalised anxiety), I was able to get help to understand what was happening to me physically because of my thoughts. Without even realising it, my thoughts were triggering unpleasant reactions in my body, such as nausea, headaches and the worst feeling, detachment. Because these physical sensations are so strong, overpowering and unnatural, it was always hard not to think there was something medically wrong with me, that I must have a serious illness to feel this way (which, of course, only fuelled these triggers more). For example, you have an unhealthy thought and as a result of that thought, you experience physical symptoms.

I've been on medication in the past which has helped me to get a handle on anxiety long enough for me to completely understand it. Anxiety is normal natural energy. And that's all it is: nervous energy; your 'fight or flight' response kicking in.

Once I realised this, I started to become aware of what triggered my anxiety and what made it worse for me. For example, mornings were generally stressful, having to organise kids to school and get to work on time. Drinking coffee first thing had to go, as I noticed when I did have that morning cup, I wanted another which led to about five cups a day. It made me short-tempered and irritated and by the time the afternoon came around, I needed more caffeine. And my anxiety was through the roof. It's all about balancing my life to live it healthier.

Depression

Unhappiness and a feeling that there is no hope. Mental illness. Although they say anxiety and depression go hand in hand, I don't feel like I have truly experienced depression as much as I have anxiety.

Depression can render one immobile, stop caring and be void of all emotion. To write with depression is an ongoing struggle for some. It can also work as a catharsis, to write out your feelings every day. To be able to express them in such a way that might provide some outlet or release of how low one is feeling. Although it's the struggle to have the motivation to write during depression which is the problem in the first place.

Be aware of your feelings and realise that it's okay to feel this way. Take each day as it comes. Accept how you are feeling and realise that you will feel differently another day. Try to make sure you balance your writing life with writing, networking and time for yourself, as well as others in your life. Writing is good for the soul, but you need to work on your mind and body as well. They are equally important!

It can be easy to stay indoors and in your writer world, but remember to step outside of it and socialise with other writers.

Get out of your head and be present.

11

Physical Fears

AUTHOR FEAR: habits.

HABIT (definition): a tendency, constantly shown to act in a certain way.

OVERCOME

We're all habitually addicted to something, whether it be a television show, chocolate, coffee, sex or something a bit more dangerous like drugs and alcohol. The fear here is whether you believe your habit to be a hinderance to your writing.

In the past, I noticed if I had an alcoholic beverage, I usually didn't get my words down in the evening. I sat and relaxed instead. It became a choice of what was more important: getting my words down or relaxing? My words, of course.

After a time, I had a sense of accomplishment at having achieved what was, and is still, very important to me: my writing goals.

Breaking a habit and creating a new one is never easy. If it was, we'd all be achieving what we wanted every single day. Instead, it takes time, a lot of trial and error and effort to turn an action into a repetitive one. The key is to keep trying until you discover what works best for you. Don't be defeated! Writing practice has taken me years to perfect for it to become second nature.

Physical or Mental Disadvantange

AUTHOR FEAR: disadvantage.

DISABILITY (definition): lack of some physical or mental ability.

OVERCOME

A common belief would be to write *'you need hands'*. What happens if you lose a hand or both? Does it mean you can't write anymore?

That's not always the case.

I know of an author (who was seriously injured and blinded in an accident) who typed their book using only one finger. It took 11 years, but that author focused; and did it!

Have you heard the story of the girl in China with Cerebral Palsy who has only been able to move her head and her foot from a young age? She taught herself to read and write and has learned to type using her left foot. She has written a book over 60,000 words long, through sheer dedication and learning the art of patience.

In today's world with Audio taking off and Voice First a way of the future, to write you don't need sight, sound or specific body parts. You can dictate (using your voice) with software that's been created specifically for this.

I never believed I would be able to write this way (using my voice) but writing is all about voice. I dictate part of the time and type the rest.

In some instances, there are ways to do something when you might think there aren't. Don't fear what you believe may hold you back. Find out if there is a way to work around it instead. It might take you a little longer, but you'll gain so much more in the process than you ever imagined you would.

Money

AUTHOR FEAR: money.

EARNINGS (definition): to gain by labour or service.

OVERCOME

You don't need money to write a book. However, if you have decided to go down the independent publishing route, you will need money to publish it. General costs up front will be for an editor (I don't recommend publishing without one) and a decent cover design artist. These two things will make or break your product. Costs thereafter are dependent on your marketing plan and budget.

The possibility of not earning any money from your writing is the worry most of us have. We want to be rewarded for our time and effort. And we want to do it over again and again. As human beings we need water and food to survive. To buy these items we need money. We have jobs to make this money. But making money takes our time. We want to spend time working on our writing. Therefore, our writing needs to earn us money so we can exchange it for our time.

As an author, I accept the probability of making millions from my first book is zero. Well, I know this for a fact. I anticipate that having three books will be the beginning of earning an author income. I expect every book written thereafter will increase my author earnings until I have over 20 books and earning a full-time wage from my author business. The author business, like most start-ups, takes time to build. I'm in this for the long run. I understand that this is not a 'get quick rich' scheme or plan. I just know that I will keep writing and building my author platform until it is earning what I need to support my family full-time.

Authors not only earn an income solely from their books, they can also supplement their earnings by using their books to earn money from other means of income, such as teaching or speaking. The book (product) is only the beginning of your author earnings. If you are productive, put yourself out there and you can make a good living in many areas from your writing using the themes of your books.

You can also earn an income by writing for other people in other forms such as articles, blogs, advertising and web content.

Check out *Freelance Writing, Quick Tips for Fast Success* for help on how to conduct yourself as a freelance writer to subsidise your author income.

hybridauthor.com.au/freelance-writing-quick-tips-for-fast-success

Unsupportive People

AUTHOR FEAR: unsupportive people.

DISCOURAGE (definition): to cause to lose spirit or courage; dishearten.

OVERCOME

An unsupportive person can be anyone: a person at work or someone closer to home, such as a family member or a friend. It's difficult to deal with someone who has a negative view of your life. It's especially tough when it's a loved one who's putting down the things you are proud of or trying to achieve, as it's these people in your life you need support from the most.

In the majority of cases, this behaviour from a close unsupportive person is unintentional, whilst in others, it stems from jealousy. I've found it's mainly because these people don't understand what it is you are doing or why you are investing so much of your time into something you have no idea of the outcome. They may not be creative themselves and therefore do not understand what it takes to produce a work: the time, the effort, the craziness, the emotional rollercoaster, and above all, the love and fulfilment for what we do.

The unsupportive person may only see your frustrations which can often appear to outweigh the good times, when first starting out in your writing career. What these people will definitely notice is the time taken away from you being with them. They might become resentful. They might have their own fears about your success with your writing and worry about being left behind, if you hit the big time.

Occupations such as a novelist or screen writer host fantastic reputations. People believe these professions to be glamorous and whilst they may appear that way on the outside, what individuals don't see is the isolation, mundane tasks and hard work required to fulfil this role. It takes dedication, determination, discipline and buckets of patience lying in wait for the pay off.

If you are trying to make a career from your writing the time, the money, the heartache and the effort sometimes don't match up to the outcomes in the eyes of the unsupportive person.

It can be frustrating to deal with these people, especially when it's the support, understanding and enthusiasm of these people you want and need the most! They are your inner circle. Your nearest and dearest. They are who matter in your life. And if your writing matters greatly to you, it will hurt when both your writing and your important but unsupportive person collide.

For the unintentional unsupportive person

A conversation needs to take place with your unsupportive person regarding how their actions are affecting you. Make them aware of what they do and how it makes you feel. There's no point in trying to make them understand if they don't. You can only voice your opinion; explain what you are doing in depth; what it means to you. And demonstrate how it hurts you when they are not being supportive. As long as your author aspirations are not draining your family's time and finances, then there's no reason they shouldn't be unsupportive towards you. If writing is what you want to do with your life and you're continuing with what's required of you professionally and personally outside of writing, then there should be no problem.

Some family members might be cold at the prospect of you having a passion, the enthusiasm and drive to go after your ambitions. There might be a possibility they've never had the courage to chase what they effectively believe is a 'pipe dream'.

Common misgivings from unsupportive people:

- *"It's not worth the time and effort you've put in."*
- *"You've spent more than you'll ever make so far."*
- *"You're wasting your time."*

Responsibilities

AUTHOR FEAR: responsibilities.

OBLIGATION (definition): a binding requirement as to action; duty.

OVERCOME

Many writers have responsibilities to look after children, elders or other dependants. Spending time writing can cause you to feel like you are ignoring the people in your care. When I was at home with my children, before earning a living from my writing, I used to feel guilty doing my words, thinking I should be with my kids, and then guilty when I wasn't writing and being with my kids. It's too easy to feel torn. It's too easy to feel you can't win or you aren't getting anywhere fast, juggling everything on your plate.

It's taken many years and a lot of shuffling for me to balance all aspects of my life. In a day, sometimes I have hours to write; others, only minutes. Whatever the time slot, I know moving slowly in the face of my dreams is better than not moving anywhere at all.

I've written whilst my babies slept. I've written in the early hours of the morning before anyone in my household has woken up. I've written in the evenings and on the weekends. I've written on lunch breaks, and on occasion I've had the luxury of undisturbed writing full days. Whatever your responsibilities, your writing has to fit in around them to work – not the other way around.

This is the way it has to be until your writing becomes what needs to be done in order to provide for your responsibilities.

We all have responsibilities, be it family, friends or other undertakings. It's called a fulfilled life and it's unavoidable. Responsibilities can take the best of you, so playing around with timetables and scheduling various writing dates to discover what works best for you is imperative to your writing success.

As more commitments came into my life, I started dictating to stay on track with my writing goals.

REMEMBER!

Nothing is set in stone. The wonderful thing about writing is you can make your own rules. In doing so, be realistic and kind to yourself.

Time

AUTHOR FEAR: time.

TIME (definition): an allotted period, as of one's life.

OVERCOME

Although time is not a physical component, you physically exchange your time to conduct the act of writing. And it takes time to write a book. The amount of time it takes depends on many things: your experience, commitments, responsibilities, motivation, determination, dedication and the hours you put in. Books can take years to write. My first book took a year and half; my second, another year; my third, five years (due to my writing degree and the birth of my second child).

The fear of time has many faces. You could worry you aren't putting in enough time with your writing. If that's the case, keep note of the times you do write and work out how much you are achieving. If it's not as much as you'd like, then work out a plan to do a little more, and gradually you will build up to writing a lot. Again, this takes time.

In the beginning, novice writers may ponder over the amount of time and effort they are putting into their writing with no obvious guarantee of financial rewards or success.

What would you be doing with your time if you weren't writing?

The way I see it, writing is work. And my work is important. It's my gift to the world and I'd be doing myself a disservice if I didn't develop my gift and share it with others.

Work out how you feel about putting your time into writing. If you aren't reaping what you consider to be the benefits, ask yourself the question: *Is it worth it?*

We're not on this Earth for a long time, so every moment counts.

12

Author Lining's Traits To Succeed

DON'T STOP WRITING

- Don't stop writing. Instead, trust that your hard work and efforts will come together, pay off and everything you've ever wanted will emerge. Even if it's not what you originally planned, you might gain much more in return than you ever imagined possible.

ACKNOWLEGE

- Celebrate every step.

Author Lining's Traits to Succeed

REFLECT

- Focus on what you have done up to this point.

TRUST

- The mindsets in this book are all a part of the process. You start the work; you freak out. You finish the work; you freak out. You release the work; you freak out. You repeat the process and freak out. End of story.

REMEMBER!

In the face of fear, **trust**! Your books will all come together in the end. Because they do. Even travelling through this book of author fears, you have reached the end. But only the beginning of your author adventure.

"Always concentrate on how far you've come, rather than how far you have left to go." ~*Unknown*

PRESENTED BY
Author Linings

Freelance Writing
Quick tips for Fast Success

Joanne Morrell

Freelance Writing Quick Tips for Fast Success

Starting a freelance writing business?

Place yourself in the pro position before you've met with your first client.

Invest one hour gaining 60+ quick tips to save yourself time, money and stress discovering the little (but important) factors previously unconsidered having never worked directly with clients or run a freelance writing business before.

This short and simple book touches upon: Mindset, Business Set up, Services, Rates of Pay, Finding Freelance Work and Special Bonus Pages.

hybridauthor.com.au/books.au/books/

Acknowledgments

First of all I want to thank me. That's right. I'm thanking myself for all of my hard work in writing this book. It was trying at times, revisiting some of my experiences with almost all of these fears has been hard. But I did it, so wait a go me!

Next I want to thank *you*. The reader of this book. Who might be facing some of these fears, but are going to surpass them to discover all of your writerly dreams will come true.

Acknowledgements once again to the Author Lining's freelance team, my editor Wendy Macdougall from Text Perfection who makes my books shine and cover designer Jaz Harlow from Don't look Design, for her quality work in bringing my visions to life.

And thank you to my heart, my husband, who tries to be that supportive person throughout my writing career. To my parent's who continue to be those encouraging people throughout my writing endeavours. And of course to my children, who constantly teach me about all kinds of fears and how to overcome them, every single day.

www.ingramcontent.com/pod-product-compliance
Lightning Source LLC
Chambersburg PA
CBHW040743020526
44107CB00084B/2849